Blood to Fruit

Blood to Fruit

Poems by Tayve Neese

David Robert Books

Published by David Robert Books
P.O. Box 541106
Cincinnati, OH 45254-1106

ISBN: 9781625491183
LCCN: 2014959170

Poetry Editor: Kevin Walzer
Business Editor: Lori Jareo

Image © The Metropolitan Museum of Art: *Mahadevi, the Great Goddess*

Visit us on the web at davidrobertbooks.com

Acknowledgements

With great appreciation, the following poems have appeared in these acknowledged journals and publications:

caesura: "Piranha's Noon Conversion"

The Comstock Review: "Prophecy of the Four-Legged," "Father Convicted in Genital Mutilation, Daughter Age 2"

Fifth Wednesday Journal: "If My Hand Trembles, Let a Falcon Rest Upon It"

Fourteen Hills: "Kwan Yin, Skating Backwards"

Naugatuck River Review: "They blame the she-dog"

OVS: "Only Her Buried Hand Rises," "Incubation"

Scapegoat Review: "Reviving the Sow," "Oath to the Mouth," "It Was the Year of Cold Soup"

The Paris Review (Daily Edition online): "Because my daughters are growing," section three from "Under Ground, Over the Aquifer"

The Pedestal Magazine: "Bee Legends"

The Sow's Ear: "Banishing the Glassblower"

Many thanks to Terry Lucas, Dorinda Wegener, Lisa Sisler, Steven Riel, Janet Goodman, and the poets of Trio House Press for your support, editorial guidance, and friendship. Great appreciation is extended to Carol Frost, Ross Gay, Joan Houlihan, and Ilya

Kaminsky for your mentorship and guidance. Love and gratitude to my amazing daughters, Sage and Bella, and to Bill Friedman, Betty Winstead, Adam Friedman, and Stacy Wilson. Thank you so much to Kevin Walzer, Lori Jareo, and the editors and folks at WordTech Communications.

Blood to Fruit

*"a single screw of flesh
is all that pins the soul"*

Emily Dickinson

I.

Prophecy of the Four-Legged

The horned things knew
the scent of blood usurping sweet hay

as the woman cracked and sang.
The hooved things stamped

the soil, bleated while she moaned,
their rhythm of foot an ease to her splitting.

There was the quiver of oxen haunch,
the slight ripple of donkey hide

when the child slid into this world
of ovens and knives,

tethers and thorns,
their lowing lamenting

what every mother looses
to God.

Coyote

1

Muzzle lifted, what she sniffs out is this

broken world—pierces its jugular
to see if it still gives pulse.

What she knows is trapped in her throat
and if she spoke, you would turn into the alder

whose branches snapped, unable to bear
weight of ice and light.

2

She knows how to mend the source of wounds.

It is not in any lick of flame, wind or ground,
or the mouth of a slow river you thought a baptism for
broken song.

What you thought you knew was wrong.

3

Residue of suffering is balm.

It coats all hearts and genitals,
stains all births with funerals.

This is why the coyote curses
and blesses the soil in her same long note.

From her howl she is remaking
her own four legs, her dirty pelt,

settling back into bone, her clatter
of pain, joy filling her throat.

Emitting Smolder

Perhaps there is a rabbi to offer paper
to a burning woman, sentences moving

backwards to jar me into the direction of the sacred.

Perhaps there is a sweat lodge to take in
the hands and mouth I have orphaned—

my soul supine, feet needing drum and rattle.

But, sky alone provides slow swaddle,
prairie, a pillow of grass as seeds crack their lullaby.

Perhaps here, against ground
in fields where the last bison

was felled, I will rise as if I was the first—

a woman with hooves of fire,
their soot and char for you to follow.

Only Her Buried Hand Rises

from photograph of Darfur genocide, 2006

From soil, the wrist and fingers are not bloom and stamen,
although the child that first found the rising tarsals

thought them something for picking.

This is not the hand of Donatello's Magdalen,
although the angle of thumb and forefinger suggest it.

This is not Michaelangelo's hand of the Sistine Chapel.
What angels were ever here?

This is not the hand of Fatima
with its wide eye open at center palm

able to repel the fire.

This is not the hand I will hold in mine,
our flesh speaking mother to mother,

knuckles telling how they kept daughters
suspended at breast, how fingertips rolled toes,

new bones as prayer beads.

Reviving the Sow

*For love of child, the goddess turned herself sow having many teats
engorged with milk, but the people saw her caked in earth, thought her
unclean and lowly.*

What your snout uncovers—loam,
rancid acorns, grubs—
let their scent settle in the skin
between our fingers.

Your hooves leave hieroglyphs.
Your legs turned mud and crust
ache as they weave
through thickets of birch,
your bristle catching on low thorns.
The heat of your haunches melts ice
for want of hearing the syllables
of your name elevated
above truffle and root.

When you slow, recline into fleshy horizon,
smell it is time to feed our memory
hoping we will turn a soiled thing holy,
it is your teats, arc of your belly,
your bold milk to open our eyes and throats.

Cradle Song

Oh, the world is soft now.
Oh, the world is only a pillow.

Sleep and dream of feathers,

unplucked, the rhythm

of hooves before the knife
rests against their throats.

Close your eyes with no worry
over who is sniffing out

your pale femurs and breath.

I will never tell you
how dry the iris can become

searching all hours of the night
for fang, sharp fingers,

even from lovers,

and what turns us gray
at the temples is our desire

of antlers.

Oh, the world is soft now.
Oh, the world is only a pillow,

and the man who fells the last gold stag

does so only out of hunger.

Piranha's Noon Conversion

Too hot for meat and gut,

what of waterweed, custard
of algae?

There have been kneecaps of cattle,
veins of men,

my bite orgasmic in flutter, quickened
through intestine.

What of short root embedded in silt,
suspension of long grasses?

They sway like hairs of a drowned woman.

I have heard of bats that turn from blood
to fruit,

of men, even, turned comrades
by way of heat under the watchful eye

of sun, which today, is an iris to choke upon.

II.

Oath to the Mouth

Shoes polished
Mouth shut
Slabs of meat
Rumble gut
Fist with knife
Dainty, dainty
Knuckles white
Meat meat chew
Meat meat grind
Shine shine
Gems of jaw
Gems of face
Shape of slaughter
Mouth embrace
Sinew, muscle
Heart beat, bone
Kill mouth, kill mouth
Mouth made throne
Over lamb, over foul
Sky and ground
Ligament: garland
Gristle: crown

It Was the Year of Cold Soup

It was the time of thin doves.
We lured them with gruel,
brought them to mouth.

Bones thin as matches
we swallowed for small fires
having no flint, kindle.

It was the year of blood-knuckle,
time of empty husk and wither.

We could not stumble fast enough
toward crumb or crust. We dreamt
of loaves never leavened,

fish-heads, eggs hidden
by dead mothers—pink shells turned,
boiled yolks gone rotten.

Garifina Mother and Daughter Tending Meat

No scales or bones in the throat, the mother says,
pulling the soft gray pelt off the nocturnal.

She remembers her own mother yelling,
The Rat! The Rat! The Rat!

swinging moist slabs of plywood
after eyes like rubies.

The daughter, crouched,
longs for trout,

white flakes of grunt-fish,
for the sun to slide over them

like a warm American penny.
But she knows rain flushes out food,

banks flood, jungle soil turns to sponge
and the belly is full as piles of matchstick bones

stacked like cairns lead their hunger away.

The Swayers of Belize

Hidden, wandering the tilled jungle yard
their twisting, flailing limbs are leathered bobbins

leaving no stitch.

The building sits on stilts. Plywood's gone to rot,
tin roof to rust, beds are laid out on the dirt under the sun

where the committed age and eat and sleep,

some dreaming of the salt of nearby mangroves
or drowning in the Sibun.

Some cry over stars,
the eyes that are always watching.

Downs afflicted with extended jaws,

shadow the abrupt motions
of the schizophrenics, the raped women,

who wash themselves over and over in the dirt.

During rain they gather under the crooked building,
mosquitoes surrounding their heads like an aura,

wings loud at ear, and in unison to the buzzing

some will sway and some will hum
to malaria's sweet cantata.

Thinking of Homelands

Mother, are your pastures
still trembling from sorrow, your knuckles
on fire from hunger, belly taut?

Your children came into this world weeping
and leave weeping, your hem never tending
their check or brow. Still, we are in love
with your arms.

There is comfort here
in this river, as thin and swift
as your fingers,
comfort while our ears lie at the crux
of trunk and root as if it were the sweet cavern
of your neck and shoulder. On fertile ground
we dream in lies.

Mother, are your fields
still trembling?

Cormorant Keeper

He will tell you
after all those years snapping necks, of music—

how feathers muffled vertebrae's timber,
how black eyes, sharp as whole notes, softened.

He will tell you
the first decade, he cupped his ears,

the third, he began hearing cymbals.

Do you curse his quick hands and symphony
while you lay your greasy yen against his skin?

Forget the rhythm of cleaver, breastbone's simmer?
Their pitch is of your hot chamber.

III.

Father Convicted in Genital Mutilation, Daughter Age 2

from AP Press, Nov 2, 2006

The scissors were the beak
of a stork, piercing, swallowing

down the fleshy bead like a minnow.
Now the girl screams at pigeons,

staccato songs of finches
shoveling seed. Migrating flocks

darken skies like a pulled shade.
Dreams are filled with wings,

feathers caught in her throat.
Her father is an Ibis.

His fingers striated red.

Midnight in the Aviary

My solace, their shudder
of wing, grinding hooked beaks
while there is pin-light for flight or preen.

White down falls as shadows of snow.
Tail feathers, once fire,
hang as smoke and I cool.

Jungle voices are kept in throat—
their quiet lullaby, subtle shift
of feather, talons gripping perch,

darkness my tether.

If My Hand Trembles,
Let a Falcon Rest Upon It

Talons will steady my shake and sway.
If my tongue stutters, words trapped

like small bees, the raptor
will take flight, bring bloodied

backs of grouse for roasting
until my mouth is warmed,

made strong enough to say
the most brutal thing in a whisper

as soft as speckled feathers.
And if the bird does not startle from speech,

and if brown and gold wings do not spread,
then I am grateful for what does not lift,

what holds tighter, claws piercing skin.

Nepotism in the Aviary
While Feeding the Amazon

We are leaden, wing turned ash.
Only for you millet sprouts from my fingers,

figs are for your hooked bill gone crooked.
Our marrow is nickel. Above, the un-clipped glint

like citrine in waxen leaves. Their feathers
streaked with fire, what do they know of molting,

hollow bones gone brittle?
Here, level with horizon,

the swaddle of cumulous is a lie.

What are we but pinfeathers
hiding from the weight of the sun?

Your voice streams in mimic,
spits like an un-oiled machine.

I need jungle from your throat
to forget stretched net, how we measure sky

by finite grids. Our pupils dilate into moons,
envy what is smooth—the ring-neck,

macaw, their streamers of tail, spectrum of plumage.

We cower from currents,
no longer intuit jet stream, or cling to distal branches.

Gravity lulls us with kernel at root.
We split husk, devour nut, engorged,

make no wing-gust.
Our mandibles crack in unison.

Your nub of tongue, mine,
reach and rotate like worms

as if the soil had already absorbed us,
as if the sky had let us fall.

Light shudders when it has to face the rooster

Lorca, from "Little Infinite Poem"

all their blue black feathers
swallowing up the horizon's amber,

the throttle from their throats

over the taunting of window panes
refracting early glow
snuffing shadows that stretch,

elongate like smoke.

It's the angry crowing from the flightless
who envy the flight of the sun.

They are unable to lift themselves
like ornaments against blue skies.

Their spurs, always ready
for the softness of eyes

where light makes its daily nest

in the curves of lenses,
in the iris that swirls, opens

like a morning glory on a vine.

Zoology

What thought
is not a living thing

baring incisors to the world
or spreading speckled wing

Still, we wait for sounds of plumage

Still, we wait for sounds of plumage
in this world even angels shun.

Now egrets, spoonbills are earth's
last guardians. Larks keep us

from malice of suns, ravens
spread their dark wings, blue with blessing.

We will not release our belief in feathers.
We will not deny benevolence of flight,

or those who, like gods from above,
watch us with dire eyes.

IV.

For the Weavers

Fibers of flax, skeins of fleece,
lanolin, warm and rising.
May your fingers, contemplative,

move by pure rote.
Their subtle motions, your solace,
source of stitch.

Slight—this is how the hand
of God moved, lost in repetition,
threads of flesh

passed over knuckles and tips—
the female hand, the male hand
in slow unison.

Between them, web
of vein and ligament,
helix spiraled lace.

Giving Backbone

I weave you a new spine,
use reeds, brown grasses,
erect cords that are giving.

Rigid man, bend like a shaft of wheat.
Take pleasure in wind that causes sway
and drop your worry like hardened husk.

Your vertebrae are dormant,
in need of undulations, spirals.
Remember the Dervish you were,

your head slightly cocked,
smiling into oblivion.
Forget your body as stiff as tusk.

Listen to the flexion of my fingers
binding straw into column.
Warm yourself from their burning.

Banishing the Glassblower

Enough of lips, spinning fire,
perfection from breath,

of vases the length of femurs, bowls
never meant to hold anything weighted.

You have no speckling skin, no scars.
Your surfaces are abalone, stretched

smooth as blades. Where is the crack,
the beveled intimacy of fracture?

Enough of your furnaces' false sun:
you love what is fragile, beauty

always on the edge of shattering
from your own lung.

Kwan Yin, Skating Backwards

red kimono—
ice melting from heat

fallen children, blood
on chins, at feet

her rapture gliding, not stopping
to give aid

her swish, swish, swish—
balancing on blades

Saraswati, for my mouth,

your quatrain of palms,
lifelines the rivers anointing
the plain of my brow.
My skin holds no current,
repels the plumage of your swan.

The desert of my tongue
in need of a honey-shaped star
dissolving over eons.
Your water, wearing down flesh,
is tumbled with silt for only its sound.

For the Dancers

Blessings for those who have no belief
in ground, only sky keeping them upright,
their feet wearing away the tongue of gravity.

Praise for your undulations, how even in your still
moments your reflex is to rise,
become a thing of skin, wing.

Bless your abdomen, its navel spinning
into blatant eye
staring at the sun, forbidden and bright.

They blame the she-dog

...the violence of Rome was begun by Romulus raised by a wolf with
a taste for spillage from the hunt.

They say her teats swollen for Romulus
nurtured his blood-lust.

He suckled from a mother with fang
but it was her coarse fur

that warmed him, his brother, toward feral.
It was her tongue turned them over,

bathed bodies until her scent covered
thighs keeping back serpents, flies,

as her claw rounded out their nest
against a tree heavy with figs.

They will blame her for Rome's
bark, the nation's fetish with tear,

mar, its symphonies
of bone and sword. But they forget

the father, the god of war, and overlook
how the dog's jaws did not once

pierce the skin of either infant,
her milk steady for the innocent.

Incubation

Darling, one moon rests upon my arm,
the other in my womb,
and it is lonely work
to be filled with such light.
It is wrenching to deliver
this speckled being
with crescent hung eyes.

Do not think it solace,
my swollen body's stillness,
how I shun
sun and sky.
Give me darkness for fermentation,
heat of thighs, and I will make
a mouth, a toe, a cranium bowl
that glows as our winter gibbous.

V.

Hatching

Beloved, tell me of the ibis,
her flight confined by blood and memory,

how feathers refuse the wind.
Tell me of her nest of twigs, debris,

speckled shells turned by anxious bill.
Remember the life she rebukes for pulse

under plumage, the small drums
by which she measures the speed of drifting

cumulus calling her from above.

Origin of the Alphabet

Vowels show us home
to the first mother's lips

grunting out the first child,
her dialect of blood and muscle.

The first brush was lifted,
painted shapes of her mouth's

joy, sorrow over coming bones,
dark circles left on stone, wide,

and endless as her moan.

Conch

Her whole body— tongue
tasting every inlet grain,

red mangrove root.
I want to be boneless,

slow, a self of mucous
swollen like a cervix,

let salt purify one orifice
past a pink lip of shell

as my body polishes its inner
world of helix to dark swirl.

Cantata for Bella

When you were born, I'd like to say
every bird sang only in Gaelic

and rivers made white crests
beckoning to bless the length

of your limbs, new swirls of skin—
branches of cedar trembled

over the part in your skull
not yet fused and solid.

I'd like to say the world
provided swaddle by aria

but it was only my body

stretched out like horizon—
the hill of my abdomen,

warm stream from nipple,
the slow settling of pubic

joints making quiet clatter
after my screaming.

Once, I was nothing but music

over your unripened bones,
and one bird at the sill

offered her quick gold note.

Foliage

The tree loved the hungry child so immensely
that it bore her twelve different fruits

from the same leaf and root.
And if you think the world does not love

in this manner, you must look at wheat,
how it divides itself filling field and furrow,

gives its brittle self over to mortar, pestle.

Green-Sleepers

Watch citrus avoid ripening, orchids' jaws
go slack over the girl's low hum of first loneliness.

Among stems and thorns, where is the hand
for comfort, pitch of voice in consolation?

Here, there is the crack and reach of slow
sinking roots teaching melodies of hide and under.

Here, there are aphids gathering in green clusters.
Buds— quiet, tight— tell of blossoms quick for cutting.

See their restraint—her knees to chest, forehead
to knees, all of them shunning the eyes of bees.

Seed-Swallower

Amber gourd— it was the first, or last.
An unmarried woman, in her hunger,

ate hardened husk, swallowed
bitter seed, while the fathers

lamented, *What abomination*
will grow, seed-swallower,

without us!
In the woman's womb,

in her every hollow
the child rooted—

all vine and tendon, vein and leaf,
new vulva a soft orchid,

tongue a tap-root.
And when the woman split,

her abdomen swirling like cumulus,
they could not keep it from coming.

Sliding from labia
came the unfurling of Eden—

one girl, her voice of loam and water,
one girl, turning barren stone green.

VI.

Under Ground, Over the Aquifer

1

During her hospitalization, my mother recognizes me, says—

the wide arms of the trees have lost their scope,
and what were visions fade like chalk drawings.

Today, the flapping in my right ear is quiet
and I heard a woman in the kitchen

talking about sweet green pears
while a spider in the doorway,

without me, wove its home in silk.

Today, the faucet is not the mouth of God—
it is water, and no matter how much I drink

it will not make me holy.

No, today the light coming through the window is pure,
like when I was a girl and came upon a dead egret

in a gutter and realized it would never lift, sing.

Yes, it's a day like that, and it is a little sad,
really, that the arms of the trees are not laden with pears,

that the spider has no need of my spinners,

and the white bird in my mind,
who being so lovingly beckoned,

will not rise toward the sun

as the wind from its slow flapping
turns into holy water over my shoulder.

2

Spending decades,

denying my likeness—
sidestepping her schizophrenia—

like her lips, cheeks,
I have inherited her need of stillness,

for long cups of coffee while watching
the incline of light shift across the yard,

for tankas, uncluttered, and orchids,
singular, unthorned.

Although, she preferred a sky
with either no clouds, bright,

or one saturated in gray,
I need the clutter of cumulus—

their slow patterns passing,
shapes in need of constant deciphering.

3

Because my daughters are growing,

grief has stained and doubled my limbs.
Each daughter I enfold in arms

sees my blurred eyes as multi-faceted.
Oh, spider-mother, they tease.

Oh, spider-mother, they sing
all their days over their sweeping,

their small games with shells.
And I lament more as their legs

grow tall and thick, their hips
spread like a terrible web

in which a small life will stick,
struggle like an angry fly.

4

The one I loved, despised, bury her by the leper
or suicide, but let her hair stay unwoven.

Above her the fox whelps its litter, noon-owls
drop notes of stone. Under ground,

over the aquifer, she is alone
giving skin, bone to trunk and limb

where egrets build stick homes. Silent,
she still seeks out the nest,

its pulse of shell, new tongues,
gives milk to roots, feeds the young.

When the torso falls

Do suicides walk
as comrades

their souls, reeking of vinegar
gone sterile? Do they weave

with calloused fingers
shawls for one another?

Only they understand abandonment
of the lungs' constant pull of breath

when the torso falls
when the torso rests.

My mother left this world
as a whooping crane,

her long neck all muscle, song.
For the first time ever, her dancing and voice

were beautiful, and she was unburdened
of heavy bone, angular jaw.
Her new legs—slender— bent back at the knee

as she crossed the marsh from one bank
to the other, reeds parting, her feathers smooth.

Season of Pysanki

I try to remember how holy the egg is—
a yolken place singing up bone and feather

from a texture of water
in the space it takes to hold my tongue;
and I wonder what it is I could birth

from my mouth before dying
the empty shell yellow?

Slow warming of my skin
I watch solid beeswax turn fluid,
scent of almost honey.

So many dead, what is there to do
but turn to the egg, stylus, and flame,

leave waxen trails before dying
the whole egg red—a color of organs.
I draw forks of antlers,

Ukrainian thistle, triangles
symmetrical as wings before dying

the whole egg black.
Polishing off strips of wax,
I rub the egg like the belly of a Buddha—

but what luck is there for the living
when what was my beginning has been covered?

In memory, Diane and Emma

She does not want this origin, the sea

At great depth where the flounder's
eye pivots, she is affixed

by blood's anchor. Only slightly,
she drifts toward the west.

I know you say, —*It is enough!*
the length between the girl, her mother.

There are tethers of duty turned to rust—
but not hers.

Fathoms, thick as generations, hide
what she wants to burn

from cell and bone. No tide drowns it,
no brine corrodes this gene.

Stranded, she waits for crest, gust,
her salty scapulae denied wing.

Eclipse

Red moon, a rotting Ibis egg—

I still wait for hatch and flight,
sound of plumage

fanning my skin until I loosen from gust,
decompose into wind.

Furless

The ground will swallow you
because it is hungry.

You are at war with trees, grass,
hairs of deep roots.

Trunk and bark are for burning—
leaves, a quick kindling.

Have you seen the rodent
devour her pink newborn?

Like this earth,
she will not let them leave her.

VII.

The Orchard

Powder coated the husband's skin.
After arsenic, the wife

loathed the trees, their gnarl and limb,
trunks made thick
by blood of buried children—

the ones who could never latch
at breast, the ones from birth, limp.

The toddlers who cut teeth
on cores from pulp turned to sauce,

their tumors grew in lung and brain.
When she buried her husband, she left—
never ate the fruit again.

Now, who tethers the old vine,
burns the broken
branches of the orchard?

Now speckled cocoons
are the only cradles, roots
grow deeper, entangle like hairs of lovers.

Trees have company of larvae's soft tooth at their core,
worms whittle and gnaw, their loosening
of seeds as the soil splits into young limbs.

Kali's Identity Crisis

I never wanted bones,
small piles left on beds

by the quick-river,
never hungered for meat,

smoke of pit fires for roasting.

I wanted seed,
germination in my mouth,

clover drawing bees

to the top of my brown scalp.
I remember hearing the buzzing once,

taken in by the thought of honey,
only to find short wings,

the faceted eyes of flies.

Invertebrate for the Sleepless

I find soothe slowly.
Blessed by the legs

of locusts I turn believer
of beetle cadences, throbbings of thorax.

Cicadas bring their bulbous eyes,
see that against this blade

of night paring me thin,
that I am still multi-faceted.

How determined, these meek—
cephalopods bold,

their threadings slow and deep.
I forget fences, sheep, their

stumble unlike smooth jaws
of wasps, their habits of chew and paper,

or moths at the sill mocking
speech, their hinge, wing, remedy for sleep.

Bee Legends

In the Sichuan Province of China, the honey bee has been erroneously eradicated by pesticides and lack of diverse flowering foliage. The Chinese government has ordered all pollination to be performed by the people.

1

Women, men live in trees, their feathers

laden with dust. They reach for columns
nestled in stamens, waxen bulbs of anthers.

Nestled in limbs, they cling to branches,
wait for the eruption of pears

they'll wrap in soft papers
staying the jaws of aphids,

their mandibles sharp as antlers.

2

Tell me again, again, the legend of the bee,
the child asks before bed.

3

Once, thorax and striped abdomens
circled over petals, trees,
their beauty igniting small fires among leaves

until moisture from rind, pulp
erupted to turn blazes to smoke—

and this was how fruit began.

Once, there was a queen
who had 30,000 lovers.

Every moment she was lost in creation,
her eggs deposited like gems

in tight chambers. She ate only royal jellies,
bathed in royal nectars.

Once, our hands were for needles, yarn,
our knuckles lost in dough,

and honey coated every loaf, soothed
ailing children's throats, their fevers

fanned by hover of wings,
bees clustered around their heads

like dreams.

4

Goddess of the Pears

Families leave blossoms, stems, at her statue's hem,
touch her lips, eyes, asking for signs

of honey, riddling of bodies though hive.
They plead for impalement of stingers

lodged deep in tired fingers,
arias of wing and hum.

But the goddess,
unmoved, remains stone,

pities the absent queen's throne
of wax— but she will not bring her back,

she will not bring her back,

and pollen will coat villagers' fingers,
settle in their dark hair.

I am tired of the intricate

after Hart Crane

I am tired of the intricate
names of things—the genus,
species of animals, flowers.

Let calyx remain unsaid,
calyx, undevoured.

I will not name feathers,
as what I utter might usher
wings toward the dead.

Let wild hooves
remain only thunder
so no arrow will follow.

Quiet the name of the sea's
creature, her fins, needle
of horn mending the waters.

Spring Pivot

I.

Forgive My Imperfection in April

This season of my mind—
always crumble and loam

waiting to be remade.

No scent of tendril, green chute.

I twine no orchids in my hair, only twigs
bare of bud for smoke and crackle.

Always, I am waiting for the fire.

Listen—it says, *you are as weightless as ash.*
Listen—it says, *from your first breath*

you are burning.

II.

Tuesday's Thaw, And Nectar

My loving is reckless—
this small-clawed mammal seeking flight.

There is such quiver of forsythia, such tremble
in the orchard. Everything

on the cusp of bloom and ripe—

fruit of his cheek, his speckled iris,
new honeysuckle. Dumbstruck,

I turn sonic beacon, emit clumsy
rings against stone, veins of leaves, skin.

All untetherable, I ache to gather in.

III.

Acquiescence

I have made friends with the cormorant-keeper
who, all day, wrings feathered necks.

I have made my hair into pillow for rancid
sleepers, and am still not quick to rise.

Faced with mortality, my pruning
ruthless, I am a woman

silent through the orchard
keeping sleeping buds from turning fruit.

About the Author

Tayve Neese's work has appeared in literary journals around the country. She is the Executive Editor of *Trio House Press*, an independent, non-profit press publishing distinct and innovative voices of emerging and established American poets. Neese has taught poetry as an adjunct at the University of North Florida. She serves on the Advisory Board for the Concord Poetry Center in Concord, Massachusetts, and currently resides in Colorado.

CPSIA information can be obtained
at www.ICGtesting.com
Printed in the USA
FSOW01n0818260115
4695FS